# Catwise

*I wish to proclaim
that I love life
to distraction.*

ALBERT CAMUS

# Catwise

WILBUR PIPPIN ✻ MARIAN WINTERS

Alfred A. Knopf     New York     1979

THIS IS A BORZOI BOOK
PUBLISHED BY ALFRED A. KNOPF, INC.

Library of Congress Cataloging in Publication Data
Pippin, Wilbur.   Catwise.
1. Cats—Pictorial works.   I. Winters, Marian, joint author.   II. Title.
SF446.P46   1979      779'.32      78-27344
ISBN 0-394-73786-5

Manufactured in the United States of America

FIRST EDITION

The authors wish to thank the following people for their assistance in producing Catwise:

The great writers, poets and philosophers who have stimulated man's mind and uplifted his spirit through the centuries, and Nancy Nicholas, who has provided invaluable guidance and encouragement in the present.

Richard Chipley, who gave of his time and his graphic sense.

Tom Wier, who helped birth, raise and cherish all thirty-six subjects.

The Burton Tuckers, who care for them.

# Catwise

*I never wonder to see men wicked,*
*but I often wonder not to see them ashamed.*

JONATHAN SWIFT

*It is a*
*world*
*to see!*

*JOHN LYLY*

*The greatest prayer
is patience.*

BUDDHA

*There is little friendship in the world.*

*Adventurers
accomplish
great things.*

MONTESQUIEU

*What a time,
what a civilization!*

MARCUS CICERO

*It is our
own vanity
that makes
the vanity
of others
intolerable
to us.*

*LA ROCHEFOUCAULD*

In that
sweet mood
when
pleasant
thoughts
bring
sad
thoughts
to the mind.

WILLIAM WORDSWORTH

*The rapture
of pursuing
is the prize.*

HENRY WADSWORTH LONGFELLOW

If eyes
were made
for seeing,
then
beauty
is its own
excuse
for being.

RALPH WALDO EMERSON

*Dignity consists not in possessing honors, but in the consciousness that we deserve them.*

ARISTOTLE

*My way of joking
is to tell the truth.
It's the funniest joke
in the world.*

GEORGE BERNARD SHAW

*Fortune is not
on the side of
the faint-hearted.*

SOPHOCLES

*He that can have patience, can have what he will.*

BENJAMIN FRANKLIN

*A laugh*
*is worth*
*a hundred groans*
*in any market.*

*CHARLES LAMB*

*Adolescence
is certainly far
from
a uniformly
pleasant
period.*

DON MARQUIS

*What a
melancholy world
this would be
without children.*

SAMUEL TAYLOR COLERIDGE

*Suspicion is the poison*
*of true friendship.*

*SAINT AUGUSTINE*

*Patience is
so like fortitude
that she seems
either her sister
or her daughter.*

ARISTOTLE

*What a strange power there is in silence!*

RALPH WALDO EMERSON

*Enthusiasm,*
*nothing great*
*was ever achieved*
*without it.*

RALPH WALDO EMERSON

Have you known
how to take repose?
You have done more
than he who has
taken cities
and empires.

*MONTAIGNE*

*The greatest remedy for anger is delay.*

SENECA

*Steep yourself*
*in a bowl*
*of summertime.*

VIRGIL

*Bashfulness*
*may sometimes*
*exclude*
*pleasure.*

*SAMUEL JOHNSON*

*The world is full
of poetry,
the air is living
with its spirit.*

JAMES GATES PERCIVAL

*To be suspicious
is to invite
treachery.*

VOLTAIRE

*Who never climbs
as rarely falls.*

JOHN GEEENLEAF WHITTIER

*Thy modesty's
a candle
to thy merit.*

HENRY FIELDING

*I really only have perfect fun with myself.*

KATHERINE MANSFIELD

*Pity is best taught by fellowship in woe.*

SAMUEL TAYLOR COLERIDGE

*Mortifications
are often
more painful than
real calamities.*

OLIVER GOLDSMITH

*Fields have eyes
and woods have ears.*

THOMAS HEYWOOD

*A pessimist is a man who thinks everybody
as nasty as himself and hates them for it.*

GEORGE BERNARD SHAW

*If she undervalues me,*
*what care I*
*how fair she be?*

SIR WALTER RALEIGH

*Society is no
comfort to one
not sociable.*

WILLIAM SHAKESPEARE

*Beauty is not so much
a quality of the object
beheld, as an effect
in him who beholds it.*

BENEDICT SPINOZA

*Nature is company*
*enough for me.*

WILLIAM HAZLITT

Avoid
popularity.
It has many
snares and
no real
benefit.

*WILLIAM PENN*

*If you would sleep
soundly, take a
clear conscience
to bed with you.*

BENJAMIN FRANKLIN

*They can conquer who believe they can.*

VIRGIL

*Who can explain
the secret pathos
of nature's
loveliness?*

HENRY VAN DYKE

Nature I'll court
in her
sequestered
haunts.

*TOBIAS SMOLLETT*

*Life is not a spectacle or a feast; it is a predicament.*

GEORGE SANTAYANA

*The faculty
of listening
is a
tender thing.*

MARTIN LUTHER

*The silence*
*of the place*
*was like a sleep;*
*so full of rest*
*it seemed.*

HENRY WADSWORTH LONGFELLOW

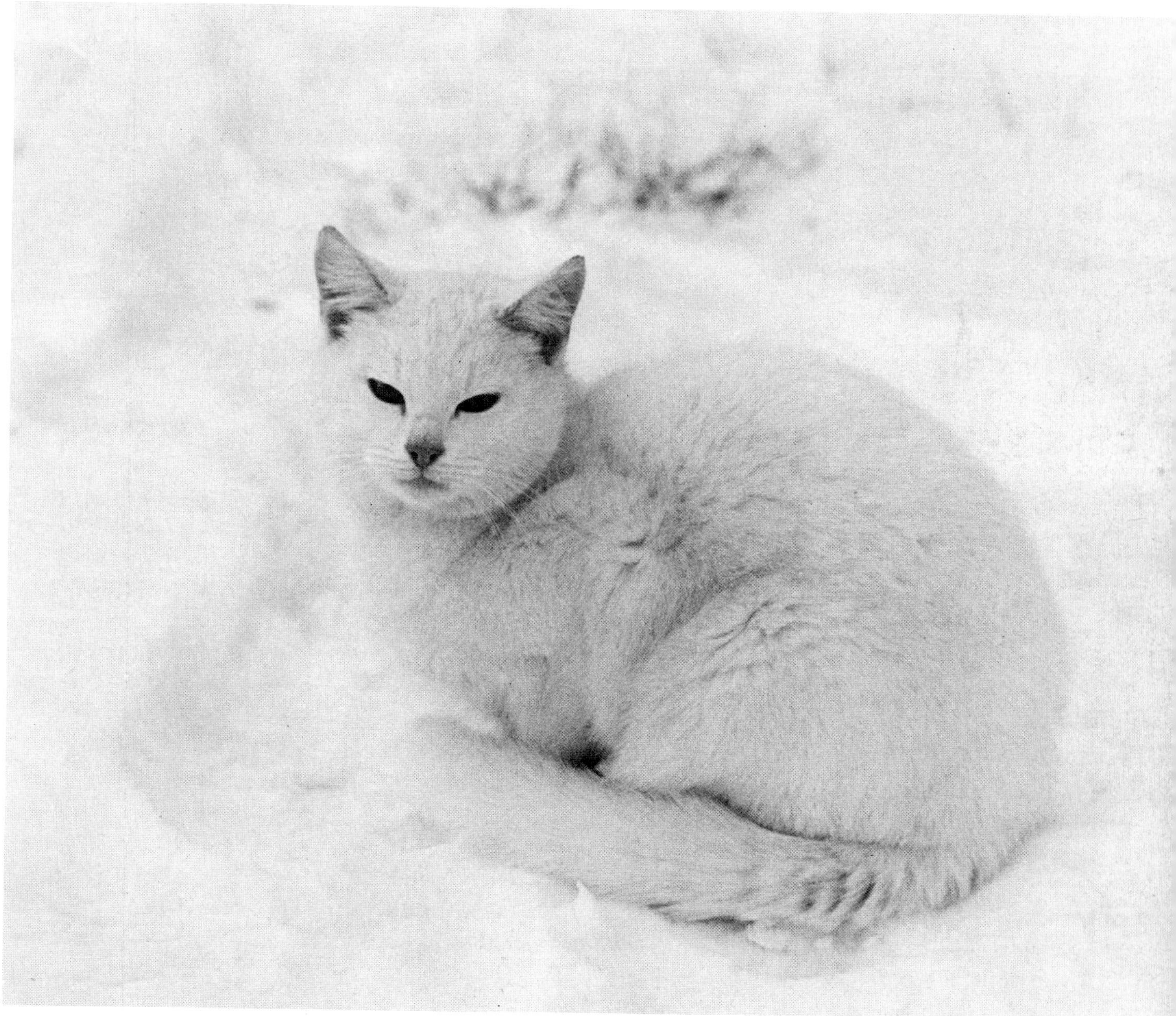

I could reflect
upon many pleasing
adventures I have had.

*ADDISON AND STEELE*

*Unnumbered spirits*
*round thee fly.*

ALEXANDER POPE

*I would choose
to make a bargain
with a good decent
family who have every day
a tolerable dinner.*

JAMES BOSWELL

*The slander of some is as great a recommendation as the praise of others.*

HENRY FIELDING

*No life is so hard
that you can't
make it easier
by the way
you take it.*

ELLEN GLASGOW

Heaven lies about us
in our infancy.

WILLIAM WORDSWORTH

*Those move
easiest
who have
learned to dance.*

ALEXANDER POPE

*Young*
*in limbs,*
*in judgement*
*old.*

WILLIAM SHAKESPEARE

*Idleness is the
root of all evil.*

GEORGE FARQUHAR

*Thirst departs with drinking.*

RABELAIS

*Every hour of my
time is my own.*

PHILIP BARRY

*He guides me
and the bird.*

ROBERT BROWNING

*One bad general
is better than
two good ones.*

NAPOLEON BONAPARTE

*The desire to appear clever often prevents our being so.*

*LA ROCHEFOUCAULD*

*All that I am,*
*or hope to be,*
*I owe to my*
*angel mother.*

ABRAHAM LINCOLN

*Where you are
is of no moment,
but only what
you are doing there.*

PETRARCH

Poets are never
young . . . their
delicate ear hears
the far-off
whispers of
eternity.

OLIVER WENDELL HOLMES

*I have some knowledge of the world.*

JOHN GALSWORTHY

*An acute observer
can observe minutely
without being
observed.*

JOHANN LAVATER

*Walk and be happy,*
*walk and be healthy.*

CHARLES DICKENS

*I never think of the future. It comes soon enough.*

ALBERT EINSTEIN

*It is often easier
to fight for
principles
than to live
up to them.*

ADLAI STEVENSON

*The blood more stirs
to rouse a lion than
to start a hare.*

WILLIAM SHAKESPEARE

*Wisdom is
very wearisome.*

*HĀFIZ*

Alice

Ashley

Bird

Bootsie

Boy

Butterfly

Cotton

Daisy

Dandelion

Dorothy

Duff

Elizabeth

Faustus

Frisbee I

Frisbee II

Gertrude

Harold

Itty Bitty

Lemon　　Little Crazy　　Little Lemon　　Little Orange　　Lola　　Malevolence

Miss Gray　　Mrs. Skeffington　　Muff　　Orlando　　Ramona　　Rascal

Sambo　　Scout　　Spats　　Streak　　Sylvia　　Tiger Lily

## A Note About the Authors

*Wilbur Pippin has been a professional photographer for many years. Ten years ago, he began photographing his cats in and around his Connecticut house for his own pleasure. At present there are fifteen cats in residence. Catwise is Mr. Pippin's first book, but his fashion photographs have appeared in most of America's leading magazines.*

*Marian Winters is a name well known to Broadway and television audiences. Miss Winters has won, among other awards, a Tony for her acting and an Emmy, as a playwright, for Animal Keepers, (included in a collection of her one-act plays, A Is for All, published by Dramatists Play Service). An avid reader, she was able to call on her memory for many of the quotes she used to caption these photos.*

## A Note About the Type

*The text of this book was set in the film version of Optima, a typeface designed by Hermann Zapf from 1952-55 and issued in 1958. In designing Optima, Zapf created a truly new type form—a cross between the classic roman and a sans-serif face. So delicate are the stresses and balances in Optima that it rivals sans-serif faces in clarity and freshness and old-style faces in variety and interest.*

*This book was composed by Superior Printing, Champagne, Illinois. It was printed and bound by Halliday Lithographers, West Hanover, Massachusetts. Designed by Anne Pentola*